AMAZING MACHINES
DUMP TRUCKS

BY QUINN M. ARNOLD

CREATIVE EDUCATION • CREATIVE PAPERBACKS

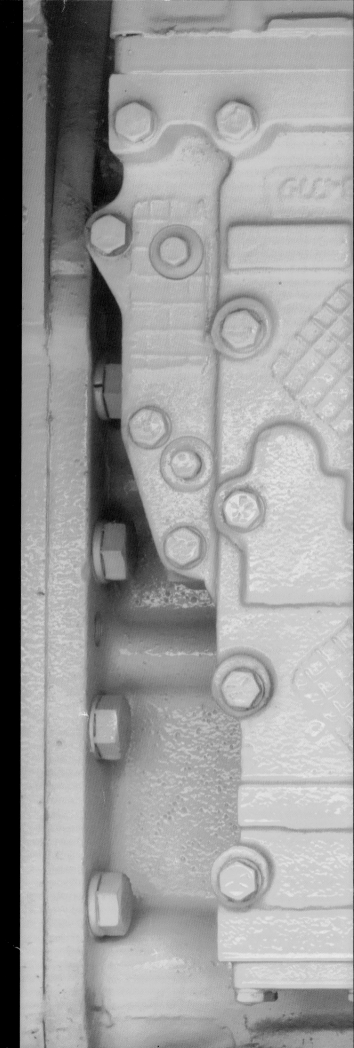

Published by Creative Education and Creative Paperbacks
P.O. Box 227, Mankato, Minnesota 56002
Creative Education and Creative Paperbacks are imprints of
The Creative Company
www.thecreativecompany.us

Design by The Design Lab
Production by Chelsey Luther
Art direction by Rita Marshall
Printed in the United States of America

Photographs by Alamy (Agencja Fotograficzna Caro, Jeff Morgan
02, Radius Images), Dreamstime (John Casey, Sergey Milovidov,
Robert Pernell), Getty Images (Buyenlarge, Lester Lefkowitz, Spaces
Images), iStockphoto (mihalec, mladn61), Shutterstock (fckncg,
Zacarias Pereira da Mata, Pi-Lens)

Library of Congress Cataloging-in-Publication Data
Names: Arnold, Quinn M., author.
Title: Dump trucks / Quinn M. Arnold.
Series: Amazing machines.
Includes bibliographical references and index.
Summary: A basic exploration of the parts, variations, and worksites
of dump trucks, the hauling and dumping machines. Also included is
a pictorial diagram of variations of dump trucks.
Identifiers: ISBN 978-1-60818-890-1 (hardcover) / ISBN 978-1-
62832-506-5 (pbk) / ISBN 978-1-56660-942-5 (eBook)
This title has been submitted for CIP processing under LCCN
2017937614.

CCSS: RI.1.1, 2, 4, 5, 6, 7; RI.2.2, 5, 6, 7, 10; RI.3.1, 5, 7, 8;
RF.1.1, 3, 4; RF.2.3, 4

First Edition HC 9 8 7 6 5 4 3 2 1
First Edition PBK 9 8 7 6 5 4 3 2 1

Table of Contents

Early ways of unloading carts were not as safe as today's trucks.

Hundreds of years ago, people used carts to haul dirt and loose materials. Then people began to use trucks in the early 1900s. The first truck beds were controlled by a handle. Soon, **hydraulics** replaced the handle.

hydraulics the science of pushing liquids through pipes to move parts of a machine

Dump trucks carry loose materials in their beds. Standard dump trucks carry about 16 tons (14.5 t). Some dump trucks haul heavier loads. They unload sand, dirt, or gravel wherever it is needed.

*Off-road dump trucks
are too heavy and slow
to drive on paved roads.*

To unload, most dump trucks lift the front end of the bed. The tailgate swings open on hinges. Other trucks tip to the side. Some even drop their load through the bottom of the bed.

Heavy-duty latches lock a dump truck's tailgate in place to secure its load.

Drivers have to climb stairs to reach a mining dump truck's cab.

Mining dump trucks are huge. Their tires are taller than an adult person. They can carry 200 tons (181 t) or more! They move overburden and ore.

ore material that contains valuable metals or minerals

overburden loose materials such as rock and soil above an underground store of minerals

Many dump trucks work at building and road construction sites. Diggers load dump truck beds. The trucks haul sand, dirt, and gravel to and from a worksite.

An excavator, or digger, can quickly fill a dump truck's bed.

Drivers take dump trucks to new worksites. Most trucks have 6 to 10 wheels. Those with longer beds may have 18 wheels. Dump trucks with more wheels can usually carry more weight.

Transfer dump trucks haul a second bed for the trucks.

Mining dump trucks often work in open-pit surface mines.

Big dump trucks carry coal from mines to **power plants**. They spread gravel over driveways. In winter, dump trucks may haul snow out of cities.

power plants places where natural resources such as coal are turned into electrical power

Dump trucks take loads to and from many different places. Some drivers cover their load with a tarp. This keeps loose material in the bed. It also helps the load stay dry.

Many states limit how much weight a dump truck can carry.

Dump trucks come in many different sizes. Watch for a dump truck the next time you are outside. Look to see what it is hauling!

Dump truck beds are also called hoppers or vessels.

Dump Truck Blueprint

mirror

cab

hydraulic cylinder

dumping bed

tailgate

tires

Read More

Hayes, Amy. *Big Dump Trucks*. New York: Cavendish Square, 2016.

Oachs, Emily Rose. *Dump Trucks*. Minneapolis: Bellwether Media, 2017.

Schuh, Mari. *Dump Trucks*. North Mankato, Minn.: Amicus, 2018.

Websites

Kikki's Workshop: Construction Equipment Academy
http://www.kenkenkikki.jp/academy/e_index.html
Learn more about dump trucks and other heavy machines.

Wonderopolis: How Big Is a Dump Truck?
http://wonderopolis.org/wonder/how-big-is-a-dump-truck
Read more about dump trucks and watch a video about mining trucks.

Note: Every effort has been made to ensure that the websites listed above are suitable for children, that they have educational value, and that they contain no inappropriate material. However, because of the nature of the Internet, it is impossible to guarantee that these sites will remain active indefinitely or that their contents will not be altered.

Index